CULTIVATING MISSIONAL COMMUNITIES

by Inagrace T. Dietterich

A Church Transformation Resource from

the Center for Parish Development

Wipf & Stock
PUBLISHERS
Eugene, Oregon

In order to fulfill its mission within a constantly changing world, the church is called to faithfully discern, critically reflect upon, and creatively interpret its religious heritage as it formulates and expresses a vision for the future. This calling involves considering both the nature and quality of change appropriate for their ministry in a missionary context. For this process to be creative and faithful broadly participatory prayer, study, reflection, and discussion is a necessity.

The Center for Parish Development has created several study resources for use by church groups. These resources involve people in substantive and accessible Bible study, historical analysis, and theological discussion. The resources assume that only the people of God can discern the will of God and thus seek to cultivate a learning community as participants explore and share their faith.

The Center for Parish Development is a research and consulting agency specializing in the area of planned transformation in church organizations. Created in 1968 by a consortium of theological education institutions and regional and national church bodies, the Center seeks to bring together the classical theological disciplines and the behavioral science disciplines in the service of the church. It operates from a clear conceptual *Systems Model of the Church in Ministry and Mission.* Its work is grounded in an ecclesial paradigm, systems theory and method, and more than 34 years of experience in contributing to the transformation of church organizations.

CULTIVATING MISSIONAL COMMUNITIES

ISBN: 1-59752-617-7

The Center for Parish Development
1448 E. 53rd Street, Chicago IL 60615
773-752-1596 / fax: 773-752-5093
www.missionalchurch.org

CULTIVATING MISSIONAL COMMUNITIES

TABLE OF CONTENTS

1. THE PEOPLE OF GOD: CULTIVATING A DISTINCT SOCIAL REALITY

When I visit with Christians in local churches, I sometimes ask them, 'What is the most important social reality of your life? What place, what group of people do you feel most dependent upon for your survival?' Very seldom have people responded by pointing to their local church, their community of faith... Clearly, the social reality in which we feel most rooted will be the one that will most determine our values, our priorities, and the way we live.[1]

Many people do not even think of the church as a social reality. They think of the church is a place where one goes to strengthen one's personal spiritual or moral development, whether through worship, education, fellowship, or service. Nor do most people recognize how their involvement within various social realities (e.g. family, profession, social groups, voluntary associations) shapes their fundamental personal identity and their vision of reality. The modern emphasis upon the freedom of the individual leads to the conviction that each person should and can decide what to believe and how to behave without reference to any wider framework.

In this and following chapters we are exploring a different perspective, an understanding of the church as a distinct social reality: the community of God's new people, living a new way of life, through whom God has promised to bless the entire world.

The church is God's people gathered as a unit, as a people, gathered to do business in His name, to find what it means here and now to put into practice this different quality of life which is God's promise to them and to the world and their promise to God and service to the world.[2]

---

[1] Jim Wallis, *The Call to Conversion: Recovering the Gospel for These Times* (Harper, 1992) p.117.
[2] John Howard Yoder, *The Original Revolution* (Herald Press, 1977) p.30-31.

The following discussion will explore what it means to cultivate-make and form--a people who proclaim and embody God's promises for the world.

The Myth of the Autonomous Individual

Within Western societies, the dominant view of the mature person is one of self-determination, self-reliance, and self-actualization, with an emphasis upon autonomy (self law) and free choice. As one of the most deeply held values of modern persons, freedom is defined in a negative manner, and "turns out to mean being left alone by others, not having other people's values, ideas, or styles of life forced upon one, being free of arbitrary authority in work, family, and political life."[3]

Within this context, religion becomes an individualized, privatized, and psychological affair. As a personal preference, it is defined by the private beliefs and private commitments of the individual. Freed from the constraints of any "outside" tradition, authority, or group, religious faith is based in individual conversion and lived according to personal conscience. God is found in the inner depths of one's soul-in the private encounter with God--rather than in communal worship or fellowship or service. The church becomes a "necessary evil," a means to an end, which simply provides the place and the opportunity for like-minded individuals to come together "in order to keep the flame of individual religious experience alive and to foster it in others."[4]

This view of the autonomous individual is a myth because it overlooks the powerful and penetrating ways in which our vision of the form, meaning, and purpose of human life is shaped by interaction with assorted social realities. No human person can or does live in isolation. Even the above understanding of the nature of individual freedom and faith is shaped and communicated by the social practices, traditions, and institutions of modern societies.

The Social Formation of Identity and Vision

Modern thinking tends to assume that "habits of the heart"--the notions, opinions, commitments, practices that motivate, order, and guide our lives-are formed in isolation from other human beings and social realities. Robert Bellah and associates conclude that this view is "based on inadequate social science, improvised philosophy, and vacuous theology." They declare:

> *We find ourselves not independently of other people and institutions but through them. We never get to the bottom of our selves on our own. We discover who we are face to face*

---

[3] Robert Bellah, et al, *Habits of the Heart: Individualism and Commitment in American Life* (University of California Press, 1983) p.23.

[4] William H. Willimon, *What's Right with the Church* (Harper & Row, 1985) p.15.

> *and side by side with others in work love, and learning. All of our activity goes on in relationships, groups, associations, and communities ordered by institutional structures and interpreted by cultural patterns of meaning.*[5]

Our identity and vision are both taught and caught from our interaction with others in diverse social groupings. The question is not whether we will be "socialized," but what kind of society will have its way with us.

Consider, for example, the much talked about influence of television.

> *It is commonly agreed that television purveys its own worldview focused on the recurring images of happiness through power (often violent), sensual indulgence, and material success. From soap operas to news, television mediates and legitimates a widely accepted vision of the American way of life.*[6]

In a technological world of mass communication, entertainment, and advertising, we are being "elaborately and skillfully and expensively instructed"[7] as to how we should fundamentally understand ourselves, the nature of the "good life," and what factors determine our "true" worth. Thus, whether we like it or not, whether we are explicitly aware of it or not, and therefore prior to any choices we might make, our most intimate and most profound "habits of the heart" are being shaped by societal influences. We are being formed--cultivated--as a people.

The Process of Cultivating

The view and way of life of a particular people is usually indicated by the term "culture." While this is a familiar and much used word, it is "one of the two or three most complicated words in the English language."[8] Culture is used to name a reality that we all vaguely know something about, but cannot really explain. It is usually employed in an all-encompassing, static, and abstract manner, indicating an independent or self-sufficient reality (i.e. "American culture" or "Hispanic culture"). Contributing to this misleading tendency, H. Richard Niebuhr, in *Christ and Culture,* defined culture as a given, a "reality sui generis." A social heritage to which all humans, including Christians, are inevitably subject.

The modern use of the word culture obscures its original dynamic and creative meaning. In all its early uses in English, culture was a "noun of process" referring to the tending of animals or the harvesting of crops. Thus the first definition given in *Webster's New Twentieth*

---

[5] Bellah, et al, *Habits of the Heart*, p.84.

[6] Robert Webber and Rodney Clapp, *People of the Truth: A Christian Challenge to Contemporary Culture* (Morehouse Publishing, 1993) p.26.

[7] John Kenneth Galbraith, quoted in Webber and Clapp, *People of the Truth*, p.30.

[8] Raymond Williams, *Key Words: A vocabulary of Culture and Society* (Oxford University Press, 1976) p.76.

Century Dictionary: "the act or process of tilling and preparing the earth for crops; cultivation of soil." Retaining this active or process sense of "cultivating," alerts us

> *to the fact that culture is not some inert abstract reality but is always in process, both in the sense that it is always affecting us but also in the sense that it is always being actively produced.*[9]

The task for the church is not to identify the characteristics (language, tradition, beliefs, values, needs, customs) of a particular culture, and then figure out how to relate or apply Christianity to it, but to identify the ways in which various social realities form or make--cultivate--a people. Thus culture is not a monolithic something or other that Christians should reject, accommodate, or even transform as a whole, but a dynamic process with which Christians should interact in a critical, discriminating, and constructive manner.

Cultivating the People of God

The early church theologian Justin Martyr, spoke of the life of the church:

> *We who have been filled with war and mutual slaughter and every wickedness, have each one-all the world over-changed the instruments of war, the swords into ploughs and the spears into farming instruments, and we cultivate piety, righteousness, love for [persons], faith and the hope which is from the Father Himself through the Crucified One.*[10]

The old implements which had cultivated a people of war have, through the cross of Jesus Christ, been replaced by the implements that now cultivate a people of peaceableness. Within Christian community people unlearn old patterns and learn new ways of living which reveal the love and power of God in Jesus Christ. Christianity is "a cultivating process that produces people in a particular way."[11]

Tertullian, another early theologian, declared: "Christians are not born, they are made." Just as the various forces and influences of the modern world socialize or enculturate us into the values of freedom, individualism, self-reliance, and self-advancement, so the church is challenged to form a people with different "habits of the heart." As an alternative social reality, Christian community teaches people how to talk, how to act, how to fight, how to love, how to see the world in a peculiar-namely a Christian-way. The role of the church is to cultivate a people who

> *can risk being peaceful in a violent world, risk being kind in a competitive society, risk being faithful in an age of cynicism, risk being gentle among those who admire the tough,*

---

[9] Michael Warren, *Faith, Culture, and the Worshipping Community* (Paulist Press, 1989) p.172.
[10] Cited in C. John Cadox, *The Early Christian Attitude to War* (Seabury Press, 1982) p.61.
[11] D. Stephen Long, *Living the Discipline* (Eerdmans, 1992) p.9.

> *risk love when it may not be returned, because we have the confidence that in Christ we have been reborn into a new reality.*[12]

The mission of the church is to be a source of radical hope, to witness to the new identity and vision, the new way of life, which has become a social reality in Jesus Christ through the power of the Holy Spirit. The persistent problem is not how to keep the church from withdrawing from the world, but how to keep the world from distracting the church from its purpose of cultivating the people of God. As a sign, foretaste, and instrument of God's reconciling love and forgiveness, the church makes Jesus Christ visible in the world. The church is a social reality that offers the resources, the practices, and the supports to cultivate a people of truth, peace, wholeness, and holiness. Christian community is both the lifestyle and the vocation of the church.

> *The greatest need of our time is for* ***koinonia****, the call simply to be the church, to love one another, and to offer our lives for the sake of the world. The creation of living, breathing, loving communities of faith at the local church level is the foundation of all the other answers. The community of faith incarnates a whole new order, offers a visible and concrete alternative, and issues a basic challenge to the world as it is.*[13]

---

[12] Stanley Hauerwas, *Against the Nations: War and Survival in a Liberal Society* (University of Notre Dame Press, 1992) p.118.

[13] Wallis, *The Call to Conversion*, p.109.

QUESTIONS FOR REFLECTION AND DISCUSSION

1. What is the most important social reality for people in your congregation?

2. How are the "habits of the heart" of your congregation currently formed? What do you think they are?

3. Do you agree with the statement: "Christian community is both "the lifestyle and the vocation of the church"? If so, what are the implications for the life, organization, and witness of the church?

4. How does "the cultivation of a people" relate to your understanding of ministry?

2. COMMUNAL TRANSFORMATION: CULTIVATING A COMMUNITY OF MORAL WITNESS

> *Christians have not been called to do just the right, to observe the law, though doing the right and observing the law are not irrelevant to being good. Rather, for Christians the moral life, at least scripturally, is seen as a journey through life sustained by fidelity to the cross of Christ, which brings a fulfillment no law can ever embody.*[14]

There is currently much discussion, at least within the United States, concerning moral values. William Bennett's *The Book of Virtues is* a surprise best seller. His 800 page anthology of stories and other writings is intended "to show parents, teachers, students, and children what the virtues look like, what they are in practice, how to recognize them, and how they work."[15] Characterized as a "'how to' book of moral literacy," the selections illustrate what are claimed to be common and time-honored virtues: self-discipline, compassion, responsibility, friendship, work, courage, perseverance, honesty, loyalty, and faith. Bennett displays the dominant modern approach to morality in his assumption that moral virtues are universal, abstract, and noncontroversial ideals, appropriate for EVERYONE regardless of religious, political, social, ethnic or other diverse particularities.

An accompanying presupposition is that the role of organized religion, the church, is to articulate values in public, to contribute to the moral foundation and education of the wider society. But the above statement from Stanley Hauerwas makes a different claim. The Christian understanding of the moral life does not reflect a general perception of doing the right thing or of obeying the law, but is grounded in and shaped by the particularity of living as disciples of the crucified and risen Lord.

---

[14] Stanley Hauerwas, *Against the Nations: War and Survival in a Liberal Society* (University of Notre Dame Press, 1992) pp.40-41.

[15] William J. Bennett, *The Book of Virtues: A Treasury of Great Moral Stories* (Simon and Schuster, 1993) p.11.

From Decisions to Narrative

The focus of current discussions of morality tends to be upon evaluative judgments, individual decisions in the face of specific moral dilemmas or quandaries. "A central feature of the moral life is our immediate ability to choose, or decide by an act of the will, together with our uncertainty about what to choose."[16] Faced with the necessity of choosing, but not knowing what is best, the issue becomes the search for a method that any rational individual can employ. The goal is to discover objective rules or norms or principles which will provide criteria to guide decision making. Two central methods, (1) utilitarian: acting in order to achieve the greatest good for the greatest number of people, and (2) deontological: moral duty as finding "the right" and acting on it from the motive of a pure will, both understand morality as essentially deciding.

The question "What ought I to do?" gives the impression that moral decisions and actions can be abstracted from the substance and texture, the flow and context, of personal life. But the description and interpretation, and indeed the choice, of the situations we will deal with are not impersonal or neutral; they are a function of the sort of person one is. "The kind of quandaries we confront depend on the kind of people we are and the way we have learned to construe the world through our language, habits, and feelings."[17] The kind of decisions we make depends upon the kind of persons we are. Thus morality is placed within the larger context of the whole of personal experiences, convictions, gifts, relationships, involvements, commitments, and history. The moral self is not simply a collection of various moral decisions or actions, but is a coherent, integrated, and ongoing "story" – a narrative.

From Individuals to Communities

The focus on specific moral decisions views the human person as an isolated, rational, and autonomous individual.

> *We are tempted too often to think of the moral agent as a solitary mind and will that think themselves free from all the accidental connections of history, society, and community to decide what is good and true.*[18]

Not only are moral decisions abstracted from personal narratives, but the individual is abstracted from communal narratives. Within this perspective, the reasoning and acting individual is to discover and form his or her moral attitudes and practices free from the arbitrary constraints of tradition, family, society, history.

---

[16] William McClendon, commenting on the approach of ethicist J. Phillip Wogaman, in *Ethics: Systematic Theology, Vol.1* (Abingdon Press, 1986) p.49.

[17] Stanley Hauerwas, *The Peaceable Kingdom: A Primer in Christian Ethics* (University of Notre Dame, 1983) p.117.

[18] Wayne Meeks, *The Origins of Christian Morality* (Yale University Press, 1993) p.6.

Alasdair MacIntyre challenges this standard account of morality: "A moral philosophy characteristically presupposes a sociology."[19] Moral character-attitudes, intuitions, dispositions, and behavior-is not given by nature, is not discovered by objective rational reflection, but is shaped through social interaction. We "learn" what it is and how to be moral through the stories, shared vision, friendships, patterns, and common projects of the communities within which we participate. "Individuals do not become moral agents except in the relationships, the transactions, the habits and reinforcements, the special uses of language and gesture that together constitute life in community."[20] Making moral persons means making moral communities: moral character is formed, informed, and transformed within communal life and practice. Even the view of the liberated, isolated, and free "choosing" individual is dependent on "a 'community' that exists by devaluing community and a 'tradition' whose claim is that we become free by detaching ourselves from our tradition.[21]

From the Universal to the Particular

In modern pluralistic and often conflicted societies which lack a clear and definitive moral consensus, many people yearn for a universal account of human morality that will be appropriate and binding for all persons. They seek a "deposit" of unchanging moral truth which will provide an objective standard by which to evaluate and choose among various interpretations of the right and the good. The difficulty, even with Bennett's list of "uncontroversial and time-honored" virtues, is that while many persons may agree in general, when the virtues begin to be applied in specific contexts things become more complex.

> *Once we translate our abstract ideals of the virtues into concrete practical judgments, these judgments will necessarily both presuppose and foster a particular way of life and a set of social structures.*[22]

There is no such, thing as "morality in general." All moral belief and behavior is intrinsically community and tradition-dependent. Thus when Christians try to move beyond their own presuppositions and distinctiveness to express a morality for everyone regardless of belief in and commitment to the God of Jesus Christ, they unwittingly adopt the presuppositions and distinctiveness of some other community or tradition.

Christians are a particular people, a distinct community with its own peculiar morality and its own coherent way of incarnating it. This is because they are a people formed by a particular story – the story of Israel, Jesus Christ, and the disciple community – which

[19] Alisdair MacIntyre, *After Virtue: A Study in Moral Theory* (University of Notre Dame Press, 1984) p.23.
[20] Wayne Meeks, *The Origins of Christian Morality*, p.8.
[21] Stanley Hauerwas and William H. Willimon, *Resident Aliens: Life in the Christian Colony* (Abingdon Press, 1989) p.79.
[22] Jean Porter, "The moral life according to William Bennett," *The Christian Century*, October 5, 1994, p.898.

manifests definite convictions about God and neighbor, about self and community, about the source, meaning, and destiny of human life. As a community witnessing to God's inbreaking redemptive reign through faithful discipleship patterned in Jesus Christ and empowered by the Holy Spirit, Christians are a people

> *who see and do things differently. They are the kind of people who serve rather than dominate, who forgive and seek reconciliation rather than bear grudges and persist in alienating others, who feed the hungry and visit those in prison without any fanfare or expectations of return. They are the kind of people who speak out against injustice, who are more concerned about others' welfare than their own, the kind of people willing to risk their lives so that others may live.*[23]

From Development to Transformation

A vast literature has grown up around issues of "moral development." Emphasizing universal principles, analytical reasoning, disinterested evaluations, decisiveness of will, and rational discourse, the focus is upon making judgments about particular acts. Moral growth is "the development of the ability to provide increasingly more principled reasons and justifications for the choices one makes"[24] in situations where there is a conflict between moral claims. Moral development is linked to psychological structures of cognitive development. Various moral stages are then identified based upon the individual's conception of and capacity to apply abstract rules or principles to particular cases.

Claims for the distinctiveness of the Christian community are intended to underscore the radicalness of its moral witness. At issue is not simply the formation of right judgment, but transformation in seeing, thinking, feeling, understanding, and acting. In other words, Christian morality is not the legalistic development and consistent application of moral codes or standards, but VISION, the imaginative perception of new possibilities for the flourishing of human life. As a people of hope and courage, Christians are called to a more profound growth and change than can be captured in the idea of development.

> *Because we have been called to discipleship in a community of the new age proclaimed by Jesus of Nazareth, we have become capable of the unimaginable: forgiveness of enemies even unto death, loving service knowing no boundaries or limits, trust in the surpassing power of God's peace, In short, God has invited us to learn the skills, disciplines, and necessities of God's kingdom through which we may display to the world the unceasing innovations made possible by being God's people.*[25]

---

[23] Stephen E. Fowl and L. Gregory Jones, *Reading in Communion: Scripture and Ethics in Christian Life* (Eerdmans, 1991) p.78.

[24] Craig Dykstra, *Vision and Character: A Christian Educator's Alternative to Kohlberg* (Paulist Press, 1981) p.2.

[25] Hauerwas, *Against the Nations*, p.58.

By being a different kind of people, Christians offer to the world a different morality, the creative possibility of a particular way of life which the world can not envision in its own images, describe on its own terms, or embody through its own resources.

QUESTIONS FOR REFLECTION AND DISCUSSION

1. What is the difference between thinking of morality in terms of decisions or of narrative?

2. What does it mean to say that a moral philosophy presupposes a sociology?

3. In what way are Christians called to be a particular people?

4. What are the implications for the church if being moral does not depend upon the kind of decisions we make, but upon the kind of the communities within which we participate?

3. ECCLESIAL PRACTICES: CULTIVATING A PEOPLE OF "THE WAY"

I beg you to lead a life worthy of the calling to which you have been called, with all humility and gentleness, with patience, bearing with one another in love, making every effort to maintain the unity of the Spirit in the bond of peace (Eph. 4:1-2).

The early followers of Jesus Christ were not called people of "the experience," or the people of "right doctrine," or the people of "moral values,"" or even the people of "the church." They were called the people of "the Way." They were known for the way they lived, not only for what they believed or valued. Christians were associated with a particular and discernible way of living and relating that both grew out of their faith and gave testimony to that faith.[26] More than just individuals who had a changed religious position, they were now a new people, a new community embarking on a new way of life-'a life worthy of their calling. Their proclamation that in Jesus Christ the reconciling and transforming reign of God had become an historical reality was more than an intriguing idea, it had became visible in a people whose life together was the first fruit of the new social order intended by God for the whole of creation.

They made the grace of God credible by a society of love and mutual care which astonished pagans and was recognized as something entirely new. It lent persuasiveness to their claim that the New Age had dawned in Christ.[27]

The expression of faith through the intertwining of thinking and acting does not fit well within the modern perspective. Contemporary Christians tend to reflect a familiar, common-sensical dualism between mind and body which leads to a distinction between belief and behavior. Thus we speak on the one hand of private ideas, attitudes, meanings, and values as subjective dimensions of internal consciousness. On the other hand we speak of public actions, patterns, projects, and consequences as objective dimensions of external human interaction. The inner, invisible world of thoughts and commitments is set off from the outer, observable world of language and conduct. Within this orientation, Christianity is

---

[26] Jim Wallis, *The Call to Conversion: Recovering the Gospel for These Times* (Harper, 1992) p.13.
[27] Michael Green, *Evangelism in the Early Church* (Eerdmans, 1975) p.120.

most often placed within the subjective and private realm as a set of religious beliefs, opinions, values.

In moving beyond the distinction of beliefs and behavior to Christianity as a distinctive way of life – embodied convictions or thoughtful actions – the consideration of "ecclesial practices" can be extremely helpful. Christians are not simply individuals who believe certain things, but a people "who engage and do not engage in certain practices because they have found them appropriate or inappropriate to their way of life." The cultivation of the people of God is a life-long process of participation in "a community that embodies the language, rituals, and moral practices from which this particular form of life grows....the Christian gospel is at once belief that involves behavior and a behavior that involves belief."[28]

Ecclesial Practices

Practices are "socially established cooperative human activities carried in traditions through which people are formed in a way of life."[29] The active engagement in such practices is central to and constitutive of any coherent and ongoing community. Craig Dykstra identifies thirteen significant practices which can be identified as "ecclesial" practices which form Christian community.

1. Worshiping God together – praising God, giving thanks for God's creative and redemptive work in the world, hearing God's word preached and receiving the sacraments given to us in Christ.
2. Telling the Christian story to one another – reading and hearing the Scriptures and also the stories of the church's experience throughout its history.
3. Interpreting together the Scriptures and the history of the church's experience, particularly in relation to their meaning for our own lives in the world.
4. Praying – together and by ourselves, not only in formal services of worship, but in all times and places.
5. Confessing our sin to one another, and forgiving and becoming reconciled.
6. Tolerating one another's failures and encouraging one another in the work each must do and the vocation each must live.
7. Carrying out specific faithful acts of service and witness together.
8. Suffering with and for each other and all whom Jesus showed us to be our neighbors.
9. Providing hospitality and care, not only to one another but to strangers.

---

[28] Stanley Hauerwas, *Character and the Christian Life* (Trinity University Press, 1975) pp.210-211.
[29] Craig Dykstra, "Reconceiving Practice," *Shifting Boundaries: Contextual Approaches to the Structure of Theological Education*, Barbara Wheeler and Edward Farley, eds. (Westminster/John Knox Press, 1991).

10. Listening and talking attentively to one another about our particular experiences in life.
11. Struggling together to become conscious of and understand the nature of the context in which we live.
12. Criticizing and resisting all those powers and patterns (both within the church and in the world as a whole) that destroy human beings, corrode human community, and injure God's creation.
13. Working together to maintain and create social structures and institutions which will sustain life in the world in ways that accord with God's will.[30]

In the context of this discussion, the term "practice" has a particular meaning. It refers to "a regulated, social form of human activity that includes an ongoing tradition and designated practitioners."[31] Ecclesial practices have at least four characteristics: they are historical, communal, experiential, and dynamic. These four elements are not separate and distinct but rather are interrelated in a fundamental manner. They overlap and mutually influence and enrich one another. Ecclesial practices – those practices which shape the belief and behavior of the church – have at least four characteristics:

HISTORICAL: Within the life of the church we do not construct our own ecclesial practices. We do not have to reinvent the wheel. We learn the patterns of the faith, the practices of the church, from others who have learned them before us. The contemporary Christian community is enriched by a long heritage of persons who have struggled to discern and manifest God's creative, redemptive, and transformative activity. The practices by which we learn the content and the form of the Christian way of life are grounded in the historical journey of those who have gone before us – we participate in a tradition. Yet this is not a static or dead tradition, but a dynamic and living tradition. We participate in established and received practices, but are continually called to reinterpret them in light of God's call for our mission in our present situation. In this the church is challenged to be both innovative and faithful as it contributes to and "passes on" the historical practices which shape the life of the Christian community.

COMMUNAL: A practice is a socially established form of cooperative human activity. Within the life of the church we do not engage in isolated, private, and individualistic practices. Ecclesial practices involve people doing things with one another, even if these people are not engaged in this activity at the same time and place. An ecclesial practice is a complex tradition of interactions among many people sustained over a long period of time. One person's action becomes practice only insofar as it is participation in the larger practice of a community and a tradition. While prayer is certainly a form of personal devotion, within

---

[30] Craig Dykstra, *Growing in the Life of Christian Faith* (Theology and Worship Ministry Unit, Presbyterian Church (USA), 1989) p.27-28.
[31] Don Richter, Unpublished Ph.D. Dissertation, Princeton Theological Seminary.

the Christian community the form of individual prayer is intimately shaped by the form of communal prayer – the liturgy of corporate worship.

The communal characteristic of ecclesial practices is intrinsically linked with the historical:

> *[Christian community involves] profound, life-orienting, identity-shaping participation in the constitutive practices of Christian life... Participation in these practices, certainly participation at any significant level of depth and understanding, must be learned....*
>
> *In order to learn them and learn in the context of them, we need others who are competent in these practices to help us: to be our models, mentors, teachers, and partners in practice. We need people who will include us in these practices as they themselves are engaged in them and who will show us how to do what the practices require. We also need them to explain to us what the practices mean, what the reasons, understandings, insights, and values embedded in them are. And we need them to lure us and press us beyond our current understandings of and competence in these practices, to the point where we together may extend and deepen these practices themselves.*[32]

EXPERIENTIAL: The benefits of an ecclesial practice can only be gained through participation in that practice. Studying or talking about the ecclesial practice of hospitality, for instance, is not enough, we need to actually get involved in welcoming and caring for others. The fruits of the Spirit (Gal. 5:22-23) are not simply the end results of a particular activity, but "internal goods" which are realized in the process of being involved in a particular ecclesial practice. For example, we are called to be sensitive and caring to one another, to listen and talk attentively to one another, not only in a time of crisis, but also in the midst of the organizational or "business" tasks of the church. The signs of a "successful" congregation are not determined by quantitative measures: the size of its budget, the number of its members, the quality of its musical efforts, or even by the amount of social services, but by the quality of Christian love realized in the midst of its common life and ministry. The value of a congregation's ecclesial practices is not exhausted by the resulting product or by "external" goods as defined by society (status, power, influence), but is to be found in the actual process of involvement and participation.

DYNAMIC: Christians are called to "press on toward the goal for the prize of the heavenly call of God in Christ Jesus" (Phil. 3:14). As persons who live "in Christ" we are to "grow in Christ." Thus ecclesial practices are dynamic; they grow and change, as we are open to God's transforming presence. The more deeply we participate in a practice, the more we are empowered to engage in this form of activity in fresh and creative ways. Thus we are not only called to participate in various ecclesial practices, but to participate well. Involvement in ecclesial practices demands insight, intelligence, discernment, judgment, skill, and

[32] Dykstra, "Reconceiving Practice," p.50.

commitment. Christians are called to continually be intentional about and to evaluate the faithfulness and the effectiveness of the various practices within their midst. The purpose of all of the ecclesial practices is to enable the church "to see, grasp, and participate ever more deeply in the redemptive transformation of personal and social life that God is carrying out."[33]

[33] Craig Dykstra, "No Longer Strangers: The Church and Its Educational Ministry," *Princeton Seminary Bulletin,* 6.3 (November 1985) p.199.

QUESTIONS FORMFLECTION AND DISCUSSION

1. How does speaking of Christians as "people of the Way" relate to your understanding of the church?

2. Looking at Dykstra's list of ecclesial practices, identify those that are most important within your congregation. Which would you like to see practiced more often. What would need to change in order for this to happen?

3. Considering for a moment, the practice of the Lord's Supper within your church, describe how it is:

   a. Historical:

   b. Communal:

   c. Experiential:

   d. Dynamic

4. What do you think is the value of considering the life, ministry, and mission of the church from the perspective of ecclesial practices?

4. BINDING AND LOOSING: CULTIVATING A COMMUNITY OF FORGIVEN-NESS

> *The position suggested here may seem to gather together the dangers of several ecclesiastical scarecrows. It gives more authority to the church than does Rome, trusts more to the Holy Spirit than does Pentecostalism, has more respect for the individual than humanism, makes moral standards more binding than puritanism, is more open to the given situation than the "new morality." If practiced it would change the life of churches more fundamentally than has yet been suggested by the perennially popular discussions of changing church structures.*[34]

In the context of offering a study outline designed to be a practical guide for the congregational practice of binding and loosing, John Howard Yoder challenges **all** Christian groups to retrieve the centrality of forgiveness within the New Testament. Emphasizing the mutual obligation of giving and receiving counsel in the congregation, he articulates the distinctive nature of Christian community where sin is confessed and forgiveness offered.

> *The church is, therefore, most centrally defined as the place where 'binding and loosing' takes place. Where this does not happen, 'church' is not fully present.*[35]

His discussion moves beyond traditional denominational boundaries, beyond the categories of conservative or liberal, to embrace a full and profound sense of community grounded in the forgiveness of Jesus Christ as manifested within the body of Christ – the church.

Biblical Practices

In his recent book *Body Politics,* Yoder makes a significant contribution to the emerging discussion of ecclesial practices by exploring five New Testament practices. He claims that these practices are not only central to the Christian way of life, but offer a paradigm for the life of the larger society.

---

[34] John Howard Yoder, "Binding and Loosing," *The Royal Priesthood: Essays Ecclesiological and Ecumenical*, Michael G. Cartwright, ed. (Eerdmans, 1994) p.325.
[35] *Ibid.* p.337.

The will of God for human socialness as a whole is prefigured by the shape to which the Body of Christ is called.... The people of God is called to be today what the world is called to be ultimately.[36]

The five practices as described by Yoder are:

1. *Binding and Loosing*: moral discernment, forgiveness, and reconciliation.
2. *Baptism and the New Humanity*: initiation into a new kind of social relationship.
3. *Disciples Breaking Bread Together*: the embodiment of basic economic sharing of the Kingdom.
4. *The Fullness of Christ*: a social ethic of organic interdependence.
5. *The Rule of Paul*: meeting in the power of the Spirit.

These ecclesial practices and their implications for contemporary churches will be explored in this and subsequent chapters. We will begin by looking at the first practice Yoder discusses – confession and forgiveness – which may be the most difficult for contemporary Christians even to consider as an appropriate communal practice much less to actualize within their churches.

Binding and Loosing

To "bind" means to hold someone accountable, to obligate, while to "loose" means to free from obligation, to forgive. This ecclesial practice, as outlined in Matt. 18:15-22, is a communal pastoral process of reconciliation rather than a legalistic method of community discipline. The intent is not to search out and chastise wrongdoers, or to purify and thus protect the community's reputation, but to be attentive to and when necessary reach out to one another in order to bring about the restoration of community. The emphasis is upon the nature and quality of relationships: "Forgiveness is precisely the deep and abiding sense of what relation – with God or with other human beings – can and should be."[37] Forgiveness is not a legal word of acquittal, but the transformation of relationships – the forming of a community of forgiven sinners.

"Sin" in this context is not a violation of an abstract divine law, but a personal offense or estrangement that jeopardizes the love, unity, peace – and thus the ministry – of the community. Therefore a very definite "togetherness" is assumed, a togetherness of identity and of life. Because the very identity of God's people involves being "members one of another," and because the living of the Christian life depends upon "bearing one another's burdens," we are important to and bound up with one another. Consequently, under the

---

[36] John Howard Yoder, *Body Politics: Five Practices of the Christian Community Before the Watching World* (Nashville, TN: Discipleship Resources) p. ix.
[37] Rowan Williams, *Resurrection* (The Pilgrim Press, 1982) p.52.

guidance of the Holy Spirit, we rely upon and owe one another counsel and, sometimes, correction and pardon.

Rather than the recognition and forgiveness of sins taking place in a private transaction between the individual and God, it is placed within the communal context of those who confess Jesus as the Christ. This is the basis for the startling claim of Matt. 18:18 that the community's action is God's action. The authority to bind and to loose is not given to just any group, but to a people empowered by the Holy Spirit to be an intentional community of shared standards, mutual trust, and redemptive discipline. Such a community is one whose members have committed themselves to its standards and to its practice voluntarily.

> *We can pursue reconciling confrontation because we trust one another and because we asked to be placed under this kind of loving guidance.*[38]

The church is not given a static, given once-and-for-all legal code, but a dynamic procedure of reconciling dialogue which offers the opportunity for ongoing moral discernment: the clarification, testing, and if need be, modification of the community's standards. As a process of concern, involvement, and reconciliation, the practice of binding and loosing, involves truth-finding and community-building. Thus the communal practice of recognizing and dealing constructively with differences and dissension develops skills and offers a model for dealing with conflict in other social relationships and contexts.

A Community of Forgiven-ness

In chapter 18, Matthew provides practical instruction in the realism of the commandment of love as lived within the daily life of the church. Matthew is a realist who recognizes that until the consummation of the kingdom at the end of history *(eschaton),* sin and evil will continue to be a reality, even within the community of those professing faith in Jesus Christ. Since the world is not yet healed, alienation and isolation from God and from each other still determines much of our lives. Because it is a community recognizing both its sinfulness and its forgiveness, the church does not need to look at the world through rose-colored glasses, but can deal honestly yet hopefully with the fallen nature of the world.

> *Forgiven, the community takes courage to look on the world and itself as they really are. Its hope is diacritical, opting neither for cynicism or shallow optimism. It recognizes the world and the community as they really are but struggles to see them changed in the grace of God.*[39]

While there are no conditions for God's forgiveness, in order to appropriate that forgiveness, the community formed by God's grace must confess, repent, and learn to live as

---

[38] Yoder, *Body Politics,* p.5.
[39] Robert Weber and Rodney Clapp, *People of the Truth: A Christian Challenge to Contemporary Culture* (Morehouse Publishing, 1988) p.64.

a forgiven and forgiving people. "Only a penitent Church can manifest forgivenness."[40] The community of those who would follow Jesus must realistically and honestly recognize the patterns of sin and destruction within its midst. It must be willing to stand under and accept God's judgment.

In the practice of Christian community Christians learn to be sinners: openly and honestly to acknowledge the grievance or affront to their communion with one another. And they learn to be forgiven: to admit their need for forgiveness, to accept the judgment, and to be reconciled with one another. And if the conversation fails, if the offender does not acknowledge his or her need for forgiveness and becomes as "a Gentile or a tax collector," the community remembers that it is exactly to these people that Jesus brought the gospel of God's kingdom. As a community of forgiven sinners accepting God's forgiveness, Christians are able to forgive those who sin against them.

> *The whole point of this text, Matt. 18:15-22, is that we confront one another not as forgivers, not as those who use forgiveness as power, but first and foremost as people who have learned the truth about ourselves – namely, that we are all people who need to be and have been forgiven.*[41]

Engaging in this Ecclesial Practice

The practice of shared and personal confession and forgiveness will not fit naturally within the life of most congregations. For many people within Western societies the church is a place where individuals go passively to receive religious goods and services. While the church may have a role in determining and promoting moral principles, the acceptance of and accountability for the fulfillment of these principles is left to individuals and their conscience. Within this perspective it is difficult to conceive, and to believe, that ordinary Christians have the authority to obligate and to forgive on God's behalf with the assurance that the action stands "in heaven." And when the application of moral standards is impersonal, judgmental, and legalistic, the fear of others knowing our shortcomings, evaluating our moral worth, and intervening in our lives is a terrifying prospect. Issues of sin and forgiveness become divisive, oppressive, and destructive, rather than redemptive practices which nurture and sustain Christian community.

The place to begin is to focus all the energies of the church – from worship to administration – upon building a community of forgiven-ness. Within such a community individuals will realistically confront and acknowledge their bondage to sin as they learn to live as a forgiven and forgiving people. The goal is to practice Col. 3:13:

---

[40] Williams, *Resurrection*, p.53.

[41] Stanley Hauerwas, "Peacemaking: The Virtue of the Church," *Christian Existence Today: Essays on Church, World, and Living In Between* (The Labyrinth Press, 1988) pp.93-94.

> *Bear with one another and, if anyone has a complaint against another, forgive each other; just as the Lord has forgiven you, so you also must forgive.*

Most congregations will need to get past the emphasis upon narrow moral codes and penalties on the one hand, and the indifferent "live and let live" approach on the other, to the cultivation of honest and caring relationships within a community of people who make time for one another, who celebrate and rejoice together, who know and serve each other, and who are mutually accountable one to the other. Skills and habits of listening, praying, studying, thinking, sharing, disagreeing, comforting, planning, working, and thus discovering and "building up" each other will need to be developed. In the context of ecclesial practices, the discerning and the living of the Christian way of life – a life worthy of our calling – are not responsibilities laid upon isolated individuals, but involve the shared insight, the tangible support, and the committed obedience of the entire community.

QUESTIONS FOR REFLECTION AND DISCUSSION

1. Read the eighteenth chapter of Matthew. How is your understanding of sin, confession, and forgiveness affected by relating it to the ecclesial practice of binding and loosing?

2. What within the life and practice of your congregation enables people to "learn to be sinners"? To "learn to be forgiven"?

3. What are the barriers within the contemporary understanding and experience of the church to the practice of binding and loosing?

4. What concrete steps could be taken to enable your congregation to begin making time for one another?

5. BAPTISM: CULTIVATING A COMMUNITY OF GOD'S NEW AGE

> *The church intends to be a community where the peace of God's kingdom begins. In this sense the church is the beginning of the future of the world ... As an eschatological community, the church always has its eyes on the end. It is unique among earthly communities in that it has its roots in the future and its branches in the present.*[42]

"Eschatology" is not a commonly used word in most church circles. Yet in a world of brokenness and suffering, hatred and injustice, violence and oppression where despair and fear crowd out hope and expectation, the recovery of the Christian vision of the kingdom or reign of God, where God's will is "done on earth as it is in heaven," may be extremely relevant. For this is what eschatology means: the Christian declaration that in the deeds, the teaching, and above all in the death and resurrection of Jesus, the hoped-for and promised fulfillment of the "end-times" (the eschaton) has become a human possibility and a historical reality. God's reign, God's future has become a power determining the present. While the final consummation is still outstanding, the ultimate goal or destiny or future of the world, the "eschatological age," which will bring about the reconciliation of an estranged humanity and the redemption of all of God's creation has begun. When Christians pray, "Thy Kingdom come," they are expressing an "eschatology," a confident expectation of the transformation of all reality, a future which has been "inaugurated" in the historical event of Jesus Christ.

The life and ministry of Jesus Christ contributed to and transformed contemporary expectations of the coming kingdom of God in a threefold manner:

1. Its coming was no longer indefinitely future, but was "at hand" (Mark 1:15), so that it could be "entered."

[42] Robert E. Webber and Rodney Clapp, *People of the Truth: A Christian Challenge to Contemporary Culture* (Morehouse Publishing, 1993) p.60.

2. The character of the expected realm was to be a new order of interactive love: God's love to people, and people's love one to another, even to enemies (Matt. 5:1-12, 43-48).

3. The cost of the kingdom, in view of its character and of human defiance, was a cross, to be borne first by Jesus and then by all who were his.[43]

Moving beyond personal salvation, individual conversion, institutional growth, or even societal service, the church as the community of those who by the power of the Holy Spirit confess Jesus Christ as Lord, is called to announce and to embody the Gospel – the Good News – the new order of God's reign which has broken into the old order of decay, sin, and death. This evangelical proclamation and witness is based upon the mighty deeds of the triune God and takes concrete shape and meaning in human life and history.

> *Our gospel is God's good news of Jesus Christ as Savior and Lord who brings forgiveness, reconciliation, and a new creation; of his cross and resurrection which have won and sealed the victory over the forces of destruction and death; and of a radically new kind of community, a new humanity united in Christ and empowered by the Holy Spirit to live according to the standard and character of a new order. Thus, the coming of Christ heralds a new age, a new birth, a new peoplehood.*[44]

Incorporation into the new humanity of the reign of God, participation in the life and mission of the eschatological community, comes about through the ecclesial practice of baptism. Although there continue to be debates about how, when, where, and whom to; baptize, the key issue is not age or form but the faithful and effective cultivation of the community of disciples which the gospel demands and the world so desperately needs.

The Cleansing Bath

According to the Synoptic Gospels (Matthew, Mark, and Luke) Jesus himself, and even the disciples in the pre-Easter period, did not baptize. The roots of Christian baptism are to be found in Jesus' baptism by John. John's water-baptism was a prophetic call of repentance and readiness for the long-awaited Messiah who would "baptize with the Holy Spirit." When Jesus submits to this baptism in the Jordan River, a dramatic change occurs: the Holy Spirit descends and a voice from heaven proclaims "this is my beloved son."

> *!n the baptism of Jesus, the familiar Jewish rite of purification is transformed from a sign of human repentance and preparedness to an event of God's revelation and*

---

[43] James Wm. McClendon, *Systematic Theology: Doctrine*, Volume II (Abingdon Press, 1994) p.67.

[44] Jim Wallis, *Agenda for a Biblical People: A New Focus for Developing a Life-style of Discipleship* (Harper & Row, 1976) pp.25-26.

> *presence. There was now nothing to get ready for – the kingdom is here – present in Jesus, the Christ.*[45]

Rather than a cleansing of sin's stain, the meaning of the ecclesial practice of baptism is to be found in Jesus' fulfillment of John's eschatological anticipation of the coming reign of God.

The Flood That Drowns

Christians are baptized "into Christ Jesus" which, according to the Apostle Paul, implies a transformation, a conversion of identity and life (Rom. 6:3-11). Through the cross and resurrection the universal reign of sin and death has been broken and a new reign of forgiveness and freedom has begun. In the saving work of Jesus Christ the depth of divine love, the seriousness of human sin, the power of evil, and the faithfulness of God are revealed. As incorporation into the crucified and risen Lord, baptism is not simply turning over a new leaf, or adopting a few new beliefs, but a matter of life and death.

> *Baptism is a training in dying – specifically to sin, to the old self – so that people may be brought to newness of life.*[46]

More than a "mere" symbol, instructive analogy, or rite of passage, baptism actualizes the radical reorientation which humanity needs and which only God can bring about. The powerful significance of baptism may have diminished as the amount of water used has decreased. The sprinkling of a few drops does not communicate the drastic nature of the "burial" indicated by baptism. Life "in Christ" involves a "rebirth," a "new creation:"

> *a far-reaching reconstruction of one's humanity: a liberation from servile, distorted, destructive patterns in the past, a liberation from anxious dread of God's judgment, a new identity in a community of reciprocal love and complementary service, whose potential horizons are universal.*[47]

The New Humanity

The regeneration or rebirth of baptism forms a new people which participates in God's new age: "If anyone is in Christ, there is a new creation: everything old has passed away; see, everything has become new!" (2 Cor. 5:17). The ecclesial practice of baptism introduces persons into a radically new kind of social relationship: "We have become brothers and sisters who have been adopted into the church to live a communal life as a sign of God's reign in human history."[48] Incorporation into the body of Christ involves movement from the alienating independence of individualism based on self-interest and competition, to the

---

[45] John H. Westerhoff III and William H. Willimon, *Liturgy and Learning Through the Life Cycle* (Seabury Press, 1980) p.9

[46] L. Gregory Jones, *Transformed Judgment: Toward a Trinitarian Account of the Moral Life* (University of Notre Dame, 1990) p.138.

[47] Rowan Williams, "Trinity and Revelation," *Modern Theology,* 2:3, 1986, p.202.

[48] John H. Westerhoff III, *Building God's People in a Materialistic Society* (Seabury Press, 1983) p.14.

affirming interdependence of a community grounded in the obedience and self-giving of Jesus Christ.

> *The rebirth of humanity requires that we should die as an individual through baptism and enter into a new life, a mode of existence where life is realized in communion in love and relationship. At baptism the whole of one's life becomes an ecclesial event, a fact of communion and relationship.*[49]

Not democratic principles and values, but baptism – inclusion in the community of those who have been drowned and given new life – is the basis for Christian egalitarianism.

> *As many of you as were baptized into Christ have clothed yourselves with Christ. There is no longer Jew nor Greek [categories of ethnicity and tradition], there is no longer slave nor free [economic and social power], there is no longer male nor female [gender and role]; for you are all one in Christ Jesus" (Gal. 3:27).*

While this is a well-known and often quoted text, its message is frequently spiritualized, individualized, and idealized. Too many contemporary Christians remain comfortable with, or at least reconciled to, living within neighborhoods and manifesting within their congregations racial, social, class, ethnic, sexual, and other stratifications and classifications which separate and isolate individuals and groups of people from one another. The church is challenged to confront and to participate in God's shattering of all barriers; to manifest the new humanity of God's kingdom; to provide a model or demonstration of a faithful, open, and inclusive community; to manifest the hope, compassion, love, and unity of those who have died and risen with Christ; to invite the world to the freedom, struggle, and joy of the new way of life "in Christ."

Christian Hope in Action

The church, as the eschatological community of the baptized, is entrusted with the gospel, the good news for the world. The coming reign of God is not simply the hoped for future of the community of believers, but points toward the future of the world, the ultimate destiny of all humanity in God's redeemed society of love, justice, and peace. The resurrection of Jesus Christ discloses that the present experience of alienation and death will not have the last word. It is this faith and this hope that enables the church to believe in the present and radical relevance of God's coming kingdom, and thus even now to manifest signs of the anticipated wholeness and integrity of human life. The church is not to be a private club or a social service agency. The church's purpose, its reason for being, is to be a demonstration and a herald of God's promise and God's vision which reaches out to embrace the totality of reality.

---

[49] Christos Yannaras, *The Freedom of Morality* (St. Vladimir's Seminary Press, 1984) p.62.

> *The only irreplaceable social contribution of the Church is the personal integration of human life by confronting [men and women] with the ultimate mystery of life, with the eternal God and his purposes in history.*[50]

While the baptized are grasped by the grace and the power of the Holy Spirit, by the forgiveness and love of God, they experience at the same time the continued power of evil.

> *Baptism plunges us into the situation in which the 'old' (that is, the power of all that is hostile to the reign of God) has passed away (2 Cor. 5:17), but is still able to afflict, perplex, persecute, or strike down (2 Cor. 4:7-18).*[51]

The present reality of injustice, brutality, and war demonstrates the gap and the tension between our contemporary world and the kingdom of God. Because baptism links believers with the death as well as the resurrection of Jesus Christ, they participate in his suffering and self-giving ministry. They are called to "live into their baptism," to learn daily how to die and thus how to live, to offer their lives and their service in the fulfillment of God's ministry of reconciliation. Baptism goes far beyond the private salvation of the individual soul. The ecclesial practice of baptism incorporates believers into the complex, difficult, and ongoing missionary work of the church. The vocation of the eschatological community is to cultivate disciples by inviting all people into God's new age: "to participate in the blessings of the kingdom, to celebrate the hopes of the kingdom, and to engage in the tasks of the kingdom."[52]

---

[50] Wolfhart Pannenburg, *Theology and the Kingdom of God* (Westminster Press, 1977) p.91.

[51] William A. Norgren and William G. Rusch, eds. *Implications of the Gospel: Lutheran-Episcopal Dialogue, Series III* (Augsburg Fortress, 1988) p.21.

[52] Mortimer Arias, *Announcing the Reign of God: Evangelism and the Subversive Memory of Jesus* (Fortress Press, 1984) p.105.

QUESTIONS FOR REFLECTION AND DISCUSSION

1. What is gained by identifying the church as an eschatological community?

2. What is the difference between the bath that washes and the flood that drowns?

3. How does Christian egalitarianism differ from democratic principles? What are the implications for the church?

4. How could your congregation more concretely manifest the vision and the promise of the new humanity created through faith and baptism?

6. BREAKING BREAD TOGETHER: CULTIVATING A COMMUNITY OF GRATITUDE AND GENEROSTIY

Too often we think of worship as an escape from the harsh realities of the world, as a respite from our labors, as a sacred time and space separated from the real world. This is a complete misunderstanding... The liturgy of the gathered community is the epitome, the model, of our life-style, of our way of being in the world.... Far from being a separate 'religious activity,' our worship is the paradigm for a way of being in the world of politics and economics, the world of responsibility and of labor, the world of relationships.[53]

Contemporary persons tend to make a distinction between "world" and "church." The world is secular (can be explained without reference to God) and the church is religious (can only be understood by reference to God). Within a secular society the church and its worship are relegated to the margins, to a spiritual or other-worldly realm, where they are expected to have no effect upon "real" life, except as they relate to the personal and private religious needs of the individual.

Having nothing to reveal about world and matter, about time and nature, this idea and this experience of worship 'disturb' nothing, question nothing, challenge nothing, are indeed 'applicable' to nothing.[54]

Considering worship as an ecclesial practice which cultivates a particular people with a distinctive identity and vision offers a very different perspective. Rather than an exercise in introspective piety or private devotion, worship enables Christians to see and to experience the world as it really is: the arena of God's creative, redemptive, and transformative activity. Christian worship – the offering of the whole of life in prayer and thanksgiving to God – reunites the secular and the religious, the material and the spiritual, the individual and the community. The world is not perceived as an autonomous entity, but as God's sacramental

---

[53] Theodore W. Jennings, Jr., *The Liturgy of Liberation: The Confession and Forgiveness of Sins* (Abingdon, 1988) p.17.

[54] Alexander Schmemann, *For the Life of the World: Sacraments and Orthodoxy* (St. Vladimir's Seminary Press, 1973) p.133.

creation: "the sign and means of God's presence and wisdom, love and revelation."[55] Celebrating God's manifold blessings, all of life becomes "eucharist": a movement of love and devotion in communion with God, with each other, with all of creation.

> *It is the movement that Adam failed to perform, and that in Christ has become the very life of [humanity]: a movement of adoration and praise in which all joy and suffering, all beauty and all frustration, all hunger and all satisfaction are referred to their ultimate end and become finally meaningful.*[56]

As we continue to explore ecclesial practices which cultivate – train, form, equip – the people of God, this chapter considers that central practice which is variously termed: "the Mass," "the Lord's Supper," "Holy Communion," "Eucharist." (Within this discussion the terminology commonly used within the ecumenical movement – the Lord's Supper – will be used.) As the disciples of Jesus Christ gather around the Lord's table and break bread together, they are drawn into the way of life proclaimed and embodied in his life, ministry, death, and resurrection.

When You Do This, Remember Me

The Christian practice of breaking bread together is not an invention or arbitrary act of the church. It has its origin in the history of Jesus Christ and its pattern and authority in his actions, particularly in the last supper of Jesus and his disciples. This final meal occurs within the context of the Passover which commemorates God's past deliverance of the Jewish people from Egypt and anticipates their future blessedness in the fullness of God's reign. Jesus' words over the bread and wine invest this meal with redemptive actuality as he foresees his suffering and looks forward to the great messianic banquet in the kingdom God (cf. Luke 22:14-20). The Lord's Supper recalls and proclaims the new life to be found in table fellowship with the crucified and risen Lord in whom the coming reign of God becomes a historical reality.

Breaking bread together is an ecclesial practice of "remembered hope." It is "not a meal looking back in memory of the dead, but a meal which looks forward to the future, full of confidence and hope."[57] As a foretaste of the promised reign of God, it is a meal not of mourning, but one of joy, praise, and thanksgiving.

---

[55] *Ibid.* p.14.
[56] *Ibid.* p.35.
[57] Hans Kung, *The Church* (Image Books, 1976) p.284.

The Bread of Life

The elements of worship are the things of everyday material life: bread, wine, water, touch, gesture, movement. And the actions of the Lord's Supper -- eating and drinking – are not "other-worldly," but mundane and natural physical processes. Rather than rejecting or ignoring bodily functions, the Bible is intensely interested in the human realities of hunger and thirst. "As a parable or an event, as a warning or a promise, as a threat or as an assurance, the mention of food and drink pervades every strand of the tradition."[58]

The style and manner of eating and drinking places the satisfaction of human hunger within a broader context. Human meals are social occasions which both express and form the identity and vision of those who participate. The biblical accounts of table fellowship manifest a particular way of life: a life sustained and enriched by the promises and gifts of God.

> *Whether in the temptation of fruit or in the promise of feast, meals in the Bible are replete with reality and are vital testimonies to divine activity, presence, and purpose. Since food and drink nurture and restore life, they are exemplary gifts of God's care.*[59]

Rather than a set-apart religious ritual, the Lord's Supper is based in communal meal-and-prayer gatherings where committed believers offer thanksgiving to God as they share with and support one another in the living of daily life.

The Lord's Supper is a protest against and an alternative to the way the world deals with hunger, food, community. Luke ends his account of the forming of the Christian community at Pentecost with: "there was not a needy person among them" (Acts 4:34). The reign of God manifested in Jesus Christ indicates a redeemed society of love, peace, and justice where God's will is "done on earth as it is in heaven." The new life of the kingdom includes the meeting of all basic and bodily needs: "They shall hunger no more, neither thirst anymore" (Rev. 7:16). In short, the Lord's Supper is an economic act. To do rightly the practice of breaking bread together is a matter of economic ethics.[60] As the community formed by the outpouring of the Holy Spirit and participating in the first fruits of the reconciling work of Jesus Christ – a people who eat and live in a new way – the church is called to a sharing in and advocacy for the physical well-being of all of those for whom Jesus gave his life.

---

[58] Ernst Lohmeyer, *"Our Father": An Introduction to the Lord's Prayer* (Harper & Row, 1952) p.146.
[59] John E. Burkhard, *Worship: A Searching Examination of the Liturgical Experience* (The Westminster Press, 1982) p.79.
[60] John Howard Yoder, *Body Politics: Five Practices of the Christian Community Before the Watching World* (Discipleship Resources, 1992) p.21.

An Open Invitation to a Common Table

Shared meals, when taken together by choice, both express and constitute human relationships. Inviting someone to share a meal is a vital symbol of solidarity. Indeed, the word companionship comes from the Latin *cum* + *panis,* meaning "breading together." Meals are social realities of great importance. And because meals express the very texture of human associations, they are marked by social boundaries. We make decisions not only about what we will eat, but about whom we will eat with. Patterns of table-sharing reveal a great deal about the way of life – the norms and commitments – of a particular community.

Within the Gospels Jesus' meal patterns receive special attention. A frequent charge against him was not that his theology was bad, but that "this man receives sinners and eats with them" (Mk. 2:15-17; Matt. 11:19; Luke 15:1-2). Jesus welcomed everyone to his table, and to his contemporaries this was shocking and objectionable. His behavior indicated acceptance and friendship with those who had been judged to be unfit for table-fellowship: the tax-collector, the Gentile, the whore. His open invitation

> *manifested the radically inclusive nature of his kingdom, a kingdom that cuts across the barriers we erect between insiders and outsiders, the saved and the damned, the elect and the outcast – barriers often most rigidly enforced at the table.*[61]

In the Lord's Supper the followers of Jesus Christ are called to practice eating as he ate, to be a people of gratitude and generosity, of openness and acceptance, a community where amazingly diverse people allow themselves to be formed by one Lord into one body around a common table. When our table is less than the fullness of Christ's invitation, we will eat and drink to our judgment (1 Cor. 11:29).

Blessed Are the Hungry

Worship is not a doorway out of the world, a path deeper into self, an abstract communion with God, but a way into the world through an alternative vision and way of life. Participation in the Lord's Supper teaches Christians how to remember, how to eat, and how to live. The bread when lifted up and blessed,

> *thrusts our vision both forward toward all of God's gifts and backward toward the bread we had for breakfast, to the gifted and social nature of our existence, to the interconnectedness of worship and life.*[62]

Recognizing their own hunger, their own need for forgiveness and reconciliation, Christians stand in solidarity with the hungry, the dispossessed and the marginalized. Nourished and

---

[61] William H. Willimon, *The Service of God: How Worship and Ethics Are Related* (Abingdon Press, 1983) p.133.
[62] *Ibid.* p.131.

strengthened in a new relationship with Jesus Christ, those who break bread together are drawn into and participate in his ministry of conquering need, overcoming alienation, and accepting the despised.

What the church has to offer the world is not a new political or economic program, but an invitation to a new communal life, a new social identity, a new way to receive and share the basic necessities of life. The community formed around the Lord's table is a redeemed and transformed community where love, hope, forgiveness, and mutual accountability can be experienced. As a community which confronts and overcomes the divisive attitudes and actions of hostility and hate, the church proclaims and embodies a new social ethic, an ethic of the kingdom. Deeds of mercy and acts of charity are a natural and organic part of the church's life because it is "a community of reconciliation that has experienced another possibility, has been forgiven, and now reaches out to the world, calling forth the liberating possibility of reconciliation."[63]

[63] Keith A. Russell, *In Search of the Church: New Testament Images for Tomorrow's Congregations* (Alban Institute, 1994) p.63.

QUESTIONS FOR REFLECTION AND DISCUSSION

1. How does it affect your understanding of worship to consider it as an ecclesial practice?

2. What does it mean to speak of breaking bread together as an ecclesial practice of "remembered hope"?

3. What does the style and pattern of the Lord's Supper in your church communicate about the way the world deals with hunger, food, community?

4. How does the Lord's Supper form a redeemed and transformed community? How is this manifested within your church?

6. ECCLESIAL MINISTRY: CULTIVATING A COMMUNITY OF GIFTEDNESS

> *The good news of the gospel is that the promise of salvation can become a reality among us.... There is now a new creation, a new humanity, a redeemed community. The kingdom of justice, love, mercy, joy, peace, and reconciliation is already being realized.... The church is to be the community of this new age. She lives in the realm of redemption (Col. 1:13). She is the visible sign of God's saving work in the world, a beachhead that serves as the beginning of a new life that God wants to spread throughout the whole world.*[64]

Biblical descriptions of the church, while using different images, have a common theme: the church as a reconciled people with a divinely given purpose. The church does not offer community, one program or service among many; the church is a gathered community called out of the world by God to minister to the world. The communal nature and character of the church is determined by its purpose: as the first fruit of the kingdom, concretely to demonstrate for the world what God's redemptive love is all about. Thus the cultivation of Christian community is not a secondary issue, but integral and essential to the church's ministry and mission.

The church as the people of God – a visible community of committed believers embodying a new way of living in the world – implies a broad and diverse participation in the church's thought, life, and ministry. Life within the realm of God's redemption moves beyond individual piety, universal moral principles, or social service. It indicates a new mode of living and working together: a communal life of deep love and sharing, which includes support, discernment, discipline, and a corporate witness to the world. The forming and transforming of such communities is no simple task and cannot be done by one or two individuals, no matter how well intentioned or expertly trained. This chapter will consider the ecclesial practice of ministry: a relational life within a community of "giftedness" in which each member of the community has a distinctly identifiable, divinely validated, and empowered role.

[64] Arthur G. Gish, *Living in Christian Community* (Herald Press) p.24.

The Community of the Spirit

It is the active presence of the Holy Spirit which forms the church as a foretaste or first fruit of the promised kingdom of God. In other words, the church is not simply another human social institution, even one founded by Jesus of Nazareth. The church owes its origin and destiny, its structure and ongoing life, its ministry and mission, to the divine Spirit of life, truth, and holiness. The Spirit embraces and fills, unites and guides, inspires and equips.

> *The Spirit of God is the dynamic, the life-giving power of the Church, the unseen Lord, Master, Guide, and Inspirer of Christian community.*[65]

At Pentecost, in the outpouring of the Holy Spirit, promise becomes actuality. God's coming reign of love and hope, compassion and reconciliation, harmony and justice, is incarnated in a new humanity, a people commissioned to make known the "gospel of peace" to the alienated and hostile powers of the world.

While the Spirit is "the unseen Lord," the movement of the Holy Spirit has very real and visible effects. The experience of the Spirit brings

> *the power of God's healing, the liberating experience of forgiveness, the reality of fraternal community, the joy of celebration, the boldness in witness, the blossoming of hope, and the fruitfulness of mission.*[66]

Healing, forgiveness, community, celebration, witness, hope, mission – all of these are divine "gifts" manifested within the communal life of those who through faith participate in the corporate "body" of the resurrected Christ (cf. Eph. 4:7ff). The promised fullness of life within the eschatological reign of God is a present reality within communities of believers who proclaim and celebrate Christ's triumph over the powers of sin and death.

The Gift of Eternal Life

The Apostle Paul refers to the work of the Holy Spirit as *charisma,* "gift." The modem use of the term "charismatic" to indicate a person of personal magnetism or exceptional capacities gives it a meaning quite contrary to that of Paul. In writing to the Corinthians he explicitly downplays the spectacular and the powerful (cf. 1 Cor. 12-14). Within Paul's vision of communal interdependence and accountability, every Christian is gifted by God. That is simply what it means to be a Christian. All are charismatic to the extent that they live on the basis of the grace *(charis)* of God. For all gifts are related to the "free gift *(charisma)* of God" which is "eternal life in Christ Jesus our Lord" (Rom. 6:23).

---

[65] R.P.C. Hanson, "The Divinity of the Holy Spirit," *Church Quarterly,* August 1969, p.302.
[66] Mortimer Arias, *Announcing the Reign of God: Evangelization and the Subversive Memory of Jesus* (Fortress Press, 1965) p.61.

For Paul, to have a charisma means to participate for that very reason in life, in grace, in the Spirit, because a charisma is the specific part which the individual has in the Lordship and glory of Christ.[67]

"Eternal life" is not an abstraction, an otherworldly or future reality, but indicates the meaning and purpose of God's reign.

The gift of eternal life – participation in the inbreaking kingdom of God – quickens and leads to obedient and active involvement in the reconciling ministry of Jesus Christ.

This specific part which the individual has in the Lord shows itself in a specific service and a specific vocation. For there is no divine gift which does not bring with it a task, there is no grace which does not move to action.[68]

Ministry is ecclesial: every Christian is called and equipped to witness to the promise, presence, and power of God's "new age" in the midst of the fragmentedness, weakness, and brokenness of the "old age." Participation in eternal life does not encourage sleeping partners. There is no passive or uninvolved membership in God's kingdom.

To Each Their Own

All Christians are empowered by the Holy Spirit. But because the gifts of the Spirit are the particular and personal expression of God's love and grace, believers have diverse and distinctive gifts: "some should be apostles, some prophets, some evangelists, some pastors and teachers" (Eph. 4:11). Gifts are personally but not evenly or uniformly distributed by the Holy Spirit. Rather than general and abstract – a mass production – God's generosity is specific and concrete. Each member of the community has his or her "own special gift from God, one of one kind and one of another" (1 Cor. 7:7). Individuals are not "absorbed" into Christian community, but discover and are affirmed and empowered in their personal particularity. Thus while the source of the gifts is the same Spirit, Lord, and God, there are varieties of gifts, varieties of service, and varieties of working (cf. 1 Cor. 12:4-6). It is this distinctiveness that gives the gifts their revelatory character, their dynamic quality, and their social purpose.

The unity of Christian community is found precisely in its diversity, not in spite of it. Each member has been gifted by the Holy Spirit and all gifts are of equal dignity. Thus the bearer of any *charisma* is called to the reciprocal recognition of all others. Because personal gifts are not private possessions, the result of individual effort or accomplishment, both pride and jealousy are inappropriate. The gift of any member "is unique and irreplaceable,

---

[67] Ernst Kaesemann, "Ministry and Community in the New Testament," *Essays on New Testament Themes* (Fortress Press, 1964) p.65.
[68] *Ibid.*

yet it can possess and exercise its own dignity, its own life and role, only in its bondedness with the other members."[69] No one may say to their brother or sister "I have no need of you" (1 Cor. 12:21). The care and nurture of the life and witness of the church calls for the appreciation as well as the complementary use of the many gifts of all members.

For The Common Good

As "stewards of the manifold grace of God" (1 Peter 4:10), all Christians are gifted for ministry. The *charismata* of the Spirit are given for the edification – the mutual encouragement and strengthening – of members through their God-given ministry to one another: "to equip the saints for the work of ministry, for building up the body of Christ" (Eph. 4:12). This description of ministry in Ephesians does not picture the church as a loose collection of individuals ("non-ministers") who come together now and then to receive religious services from professional ministers.. It assumes a community of people witnessing to the new life of God's kingdom by surfacing, confronting, and overcoming the divisions, conflicts, and injustices of daily life through their own communal faith and worship, life, and practice. It is because of the complexity and the significance of this witness that the ministry of all of God's gifted people – apostles, prophets, teachers, workers of miracles, healers, helpers, administrators, discerners of spirits, speakers in tongues and their interpreters – is so urgently needed.

There is no complete or definitive list of gifts in the New Testament, for this would restrict God's freedom to "resource," in a creative and appropriate manner, particular communities within their concrete situation. But that does not mean there is no order or criteria for the discernment and use of gifts. The "fruit of the Spirit" and in particular love provide the context within which the *charismata* are exercised: "Make love your aim and earnestly desire the spiritual gifts" (1 Cor. 14:1). While there is a variety of gifts, and some may be more relevant at a given moment than others, the fruit of the Spirit – love, joy, peace, patience, kindness, goodness, faithfulness, gentleness, self-control (Gal. 5:22) – is the underlying common denominator that enables particular gifts to be used for the edification – the common good – of the whole community.

Conclusion

This description of a community of giftedness engaged in the ecclesial practice of ministry does not fit easily or comfortably within the contemporary understanding and experience of church. It calls for a reorientation of the notion of ministry, as well as changes in the expectations and level of involvement of members of the community. Yet the contemporary expression of loneliness and alienation, the growing disillusion and cynicism, and the current hunger for and experimentation with various forms of "community," may

---

[69] John Howard Yoder, *Body Politics: Five Practices of the Christian Community Before the Watching World* (Discipleship Resources, 1992) p.49.

indicate more openness and receptivity to this vision of the church than is often recognized. The opportunity for churches is to seize the moment, to discern the movement of God's Spirit in their midst, to reclaim the biblical image of the church as a reconciled and reconciling people, and to seek to cultivate gifted communities of the Holy Spirit. Such communities would represent a powerful and meaningful sign of love and hope by discerning how, in the midst of the turmoil of the present moment, they can point to new possibilities and give shape to them.

QUESTIONS FOR REFLECTION AND DISCUSSION

1. Read the first chapter of Colossians. What does it mean to say that the church "lives in the realm of redemption"?

2. How is your understanding of gifts of the Spirit affected by relating them to the gift of eternal life?

3. What are the implications for the practice of ministry if all Christians are gifted for ministry?

4. Where do you see possibilities for cultivating your congregation as a community of giftedness?

8. COMMUNAL DECISION-MAKING: CULTIVATING A COMMUNITY OF DISCERNMENT

> *The church is God's most important institution on earth. The church is the social agent that most significantly shapes and forms the character of Christians. And the church is the primary vehicle of God's grace and salvation for a waiting, desperate world.*[70]

The discussion of ecclesial practices within previous chapters has recognized that for many people the Christian life is viewed from an individualistic or, at best, an organizational, but rarely from a communal perspective. Yet the claim has been made that to be true to its divine mission – to discern and participate in God's redemptive activity in the midst of the alienating and destructive forces of our day – the church is called to become for Christians the most central, foundational unit of societal life.[71] As a people who pray "thy kingdom come, thy will be done, on earth as it is in heaven," the church is to be an embodied social manifestation – even though not yet perfected – of God's inbreaking reign of love and reconciliation, joy and freedom, peace and justice.

The quality, character, and witness of Christian community is determined by the social or ecclesial practices which shape, train, equip, guide – cultivate – the identity, vision, and purpose of a particular people. The practice of communal confession and forgiveness cultivates a community of shared standards, mutual trust, and redemptive discipline. The practice of breaking bread together cultivates a community of gratitude and generosity in solidarity with the hungry, dispossessed, and marginalized. The practice of baptism cultivates a community of reconciliation and interdependence where the barriers which separate and divide people are dissolved. The practice of ecclesial ministry cultivates a community of giftedness which affirms the unique and important contribution of all members to the edification – upbuilding – of the community.

---

[70] Rodney Clapp, *Families at the Crossroads: Beyond Traditional and Modern Options* (InterVarsity Press, 1993) p.69.
[71] John H. Westerhoff, *Living the Faith Community: The Church That Makes a Difference* (Harper & Row, 1985) p.9.

These practices share a common pattern:

1. They are not esoteric or mysterious, but involve ordinary human behavior: listening and caring, eating and drinking, joining and sharing, teaching and serving.

2. They do not relate to an abstract religious realm, but to the very real challenges of contemporary moral and social issues: destructive conflict, economic injustice, social inequality, lack of personal dignity and esteem.

3. It is the doing of these practices that makes a church body what it is: they shape and reflect the belief, commitment, and action of a particular community.

4. They have a communal meaning from the outset: by their very nature they are social, visible, practical, and public.

5. Most important, all of these ecclesial practices are derived from, are dependent upon, and participate in the redemptive ministry of Jesus Christ.

Through the transforming movement of the Holy Spirit they exhibit the "incarnation" of divine activity within human activity.

> *They are actions of God, in and with, through and under what men and women do. Where they are happening the people of God is real in the world*[72]

To conclude this five-part discussion of ecclesial practices, we turn to a consideration of communal decision-making, to how communities of God's people discern the will of God for their common life and shared ministry.

A Discerning Community

If attention is given to the processes of decision-making within the church, it is usually viewed as an organizational rather than a theological concern. For the most part it is assumed that democratic processes – one person, one vote – are the best way to make decisions. Yet the presuppositions behind adversarial win/lose debates, parliamentary maneuvers, special interest group lobbying, and majority rule are seldom examined. These processes are grounded more in the modern commitment to individual autonomy and freedom, the suspicion of power and influence, and the importance of maximizing and protecting personal preferences, than in the movement of God's Spirit among the people of

---

[72] John Howard Yoder, *Body Politics: Five Practices of the Christian Community Before the Watching World* (Discipleship Resources, 1992) p.73.

God. Church meetings, small and large, tend to reflect the conflicts and the inadequacies of the decision-making processes of secular society, rather than offering an alternative – and more scriptural – mode of sharing insights, considering diverse perspectives, building trust, discovering wisdom, achieving substantive consensus, and acting decisively.

Discernment is a process of sorting, distinguishing, evaluating, of sifting among competing stimuli, demands, longings, desires, needs, and influences, in order to determine which are of God and which are not. To discern is to prove (test) "what is of the will of God – what is good and acceptable and perfect" (Rom. 12:2). Thus the goal of decision-making in the church is not simply to discover the will of the community, but together to discern the will of God. It is the role of the Spirit to convict, convince, and lead those who profess faith in Jesus Christ into God's truth. But because God acts and speaks in and through the ambiguous circumstances of worldly life, cautious, attentive, and humble discernment is required. Not only the Holy Spirit, but destructive forces operate and multiply within communities. As the *ecclesia* of God, a people gathered to be about God's "business," the church is called to a way of making decisions which articulates and is consistent with this identity: a way of listening, hearing, testing, planning, and obeying together in the power of the Holy Spirit.

The "Pneumocratic" Nature of Christian Community

The practice of communal decision-making assumes a community of giftedness: all have received gifts of the Holy Spirit to be used for the edification, encouragement, and consolation of the entire body. Thus it is important for all to be involved in the process of discerning what God requires of them. The Apostle Paul continually insists that every member of the body of Christ has the responsibility to share the particular insights she or he has been given. All are called "to instruct one another" (Rom. 15:14), to speak God's word "so that all may learn and all be encouraged" (1 Cor. 14:31), to "teach and admonish one another in all wisdom" (Col. 3:16), for it is through "speaking the truth in love" that they are to "grow up in every way into him who is the head, into Christ" (Eph. 4:15). So the most characteristic setting in which the community receives guidance is when Christians assemble to share and evaluate the gifts given to them. Here in a variety of complementary ways, guidance is conveyed through each to all, and through all to each[73]

Discerning communities are not hierarchical in structure, but neither are they egalitarian. Because all are given gifts to contribute to the common good, everyone has the right and the obligation to participate authoritatively in decisions of faith and practice. Yet because the Spirit distributes different gifts, responsibilities, and functions there is also an element of differentiation. The focus is not upon the prerogatives of designated leaders, or upon the equal privileges of members, but upon corporate responsibility for discerning the wisdom

[73] Robert Banks, *Paul's Idea of Community: The Early House Churches in Their Historical Setting* (Eerdmans, 1980) p.141.

and prompting of the Holy Spirit. Thus communities of "giftedness" are neither autocratic (the rule of one) nor democratic (the rule of the people) but "pneumocratic" (the rule of the Holy Spirit). Authority within the body of Christ is found neither in particular status nor in majority opinion, but is dispersed throughout the whole membership through the illumination and empowerment of the Spirit. None are given advantage; all are equipped for service. The image is of a participatory community earnestly expecting and seeking the guidance of the Holy Spirit in their midst, utilizing the diverse gifts of all members, "testing the spirits to see whether they are from God" (1 John 4:1), and willing to be bound by what is decided.

Spirit-Moved Deliberation

Most church meetings do not deal with the vital or relevant challenges of life and faith. Worship, prayer, Bible study, missional concerns, mutual support, sharing of personal and communal issues occur elsewhere. Due to perceived limitations of time and energy, the goal is to get through the agenda as quickly as possible. Uncritical compliance (going along with recommendations of the leader), easy compromise (seeking the lowest common denominator), or majority rule (overriding minority voices) are considered the most efficient ways to make decisions. Yet if God's people are called to discern and then to participate in God's creative, redemptive, and transformative activity within the concrete circumstances of modern life, a much different approach is needed. God's will and God's truth can not be legislated by prudent and rational decisions, but through open conversation which expects to hear and listens for the Spirit in the midst of communal dialogue. The Holy Spirit works through group processes – the interaction of two or three gathered together in the name of Jesus Christ.

As with all other ecclesial practices, communal decision-making both assumes and creates an intentional community of believers, a community that recognizes the need for the gifts and insights of all members to shape and guide a faithful and effective ministry and mission. Only then will members make the effort to set aside the necessary time to listen, share, study, struggle, pray, and plan together in the continual search for God's truth. Opening themselves to the challenge of seeking God's wisdom in the midst of the community's lived experience, members will be eager to discover the insights of their brothers and sisters as they bring the issue under deliberation into conversation with Scripture and Christian tradition. The feelings and commitments of all members will be affirmed and taken into consideration as they collect and carefully analyze all the available evidence relating to the issue. Diversity of opinion and even conflict will be utilized to enrich and strengthen the discussion as they talk with one another in frankness and honesty. And a discerning community will not rush to judgment, but will know the importance of waiting upon the Spirit in silence and prayer.

Having participated in a communal decision-making process of open dialogue, critical reflection, genuine respect, mutual trust, and active collaboration, members pledge themselves to live out together the conclusions they reach. Within a discerning community when a decision

> *has been prayerfully tested with the authority of Scripture and the presence of the living Christ, seriously taking into account subjective feelings, factual evidence, and the testimony of other Christians and tradition, and the result is a deep sense of peace, love, joy, and humility, we can trust that we have discerned God's will.*[74]

[74] Arthur G. Gish, *Living in Christian Community* (Herald Press, 1979) p.130.

QUESTIONS FOR REFLECTION AND DISCUSSION

1. What insights have you gained about your ministry from the discussion of ecclesial practices?

2. How does communal discernment differ from democratic decision-making processes? How do the results compare?

3. What would be affirmed and what would be changed in order for "corporate responsibility" to become a reality within the church?

4. How does "Spirit-moved deliberation" compare with the decision-making processes of your church organization?

9. IN SPIRIT AND IN TRUTH: CULTIVATING A WORSHIPING COMMUNITY

> *There is no reason for the existence of the church except to symbolize the future of the divine kingdom that Jesus came to proclaim. This explains in what specific sense worship is in the center of life of the church: the worship of the Christian community anticipates and symbolically celebrates the praise of God's glory that will be consummated in the eschatological renewal of all creation in the new Jerusalem.*[75]

The moral witness of Christian communities is not moralistic (dependent upon human intentions and actions) nor is it legalistic (dependent upon rules and regulations) but eschatological. Christian morality expresses a dynamic vision which looks to the future, to the *eschaton* (the "end-time"), when God's will will be done "on earth as it is in heaven." The paradoxical declaration of the gospel is that this future transformation of life – God's perfect society of love, joy, and peace – has become a present reality in the historical event of Jesus Christ. Through his ministry, death, and resurrection and the outpouring of the Holy Spirit, the eschatological age – life as God intends it to be – has been inaugurated. As a community of faith and hope which has "its roots in the future and its branches in the present,"[76] the mission of the church is to celebrate, to announce, and to embody in this world the life of the ""'world to come."

In a time of experimentation with alternative forms of worship whereby congregations seek to make worship more understandable, meaningful, and relevant to "secular" people, it is important to reflect upon the nature and purpose of Christian worship. Within an eschatological perspective, worship is not simply one function of the church, but actually constitutes the church as "a chosen race, a royal priesthood, a holy nation, God's own people" (1 Peter 2:9a). Moving beyond meeting culturally defined "felt" needs, Christians gather to "incarnate" the vision of social transformation expressed in the Sermon on the Mount; the Way of Jesus, the Way of the Kingdom, the Way of Righteousness, the Way of

---

[75] Wolfhart Pannenberg, *Christian Spirituality* (Westminster Press, 1983) p.36.
[76] John D. Zizoulas, *Being as Communion* (St. Vladimir's Seminary Press, 1985) p.59.

Discipleship. As a people committed to living by the promise of the new order in the midst of the old order, the Christian community gathers to remember, to anticipate, and to model the redeemed life of God's new creation. In other words, to "proclaim the mighty acts of him who called you out of darkness into his marvelous light" (1 Peter 2:9b).

Worship as Nourishing the Individual

The usual identification of "church" is the coming together of individuals in a particular place at least once a week for "worship." These gatherings may be large or small, growing or shrinking, boisterous or solemn, plain or splendid. The services take different shape and people gather to worship for a variety of reasons: devotion to God, a sense of duty or guilt, for personal or mutual support, from habit or routine. This approach reflects a secular understanding of religion as one among many aspects or spheres of life. Religion is relegated to the "sublime" or the "ultimate" where it can have no effect upon "real" life, except as it relates to the so-called religious needs of the individual.

Within this perspective where religion is expected to provide "help," worship fulfills an instrumental function, be it character building, peace of mind, a "peak" spiritual experience, or assurance of eternal salvation. Thus forms and language are sought which will reflect and be understandable and appropriate to the needs and aspirations of the contemporary person. Taking a pragmatic approach, the goal is to be "user-friendly," to attract and hold secular men and women by providing worship experiences which offer personal meaning, instruction, comfort, consolation, or stimulation. This domesticated and privatized view of worship can peacefully coexist with any secular perspective. "Having nothing to reveal about world and matter, about time and nature, this idea and this experience of worship 'disturb' nothing, question nothing, challenge nothing, are indeed 'applicable' to nothing.[77] The church is called to be sensitive to and engaged with the needs and quests of modern persons, but also to move beneath the surface, to question presuppositions, and to expand their horizons.

Worship as Mutual Edification

For many contemporary Christians worship has become a spectator sport. The ideal image of Sunday morning is a large audience seated in the impersonal atmosphere of an auditorium, being ministered to by professionals who provide enlightening, dramatic, and even entertaining performances. (With televangelism persons do not even have to leave the isolation and comfort of their own living rooms.) More a passive consumer than an active member of the body, each person participates to the degree with which he or she feels comfortable. The success or validity of the worship experience depends upon how well it meets the self-defined needs and expectations of the individual worshiper. Focusing on

---

[77] Alexander Schmemann, *For the Life of the World: Sacraments and Orthodoxy* (St. Vladimir's Seminary Press, 1973) p.133.

personal satisfaction rather than on the public proclamation of the gospel of Jesus Christ, "worship is seen as directed toward human ends rather than the glorification of God."[78]

This orientation is very different from the New Testament's picture of what happens when Christians come together. For the Apostle Paul the primary goal is **mutual** edification, the sharing of gifts of the Holy Spirit with one another for the building up and strengthening of the disciple community. In the one specific description of worship in the New Testament, he counsels the Corinthians: "When you come together, each one has a hymn, a lesson, a revelation, a tongue, or an interpretation. Let all things be done for building up" (1 Cor. 14:26). The principal focus here is not private nourishment or enjoyment, but the visible, active, and corporate "priesthood of all believers" nurturing and utilizing their gifts in mutual ministry in order "to equip the saints for the work of ministry, for building up the body of Christ" (Eph. 4:12).

Worship as A Way of Life

Paul's understanding of what happens when Christians gather reflects his belief that in Jesus Christ the distinction between the sacred and the profane has been overcome. All of life, indeed all of created reality, has been redeemed and called into God's service. While Christians praise God in their communal gatherings, worship is finally to be expressed in the whole of their lives. Thus worship knows no special place or time but is a wholistic experience. Although using the cultic language through which Jewish worship was offered in the Temple, Paul applies this language metaphorically to the sphere of everyday behavior. In the totality of their lives Christians are to offer honor and thanksgiving to God: "by the mercies of God, present your bodies as a living sacrifice, holy and acceptable to God, which is your spiritual worship" (Rom. 12:1). Believers worship God, acceptably or unacceptably, in whatever they do in their entire way of life.

Encompassing but moving beyond specific ritual activity, worship designates the calling and forming of a people who through their very way of life offer praise to the glory of God. Worship symbolizes the redemption and fulfillment of life, the wholeness of life as intended by God.

> *In practice this means behaving in such a way that God's will, which is by definition good and perfect, determines all their actions – something that can only be achieved if their minds accept God's standards, rather than those characteristic of the times in which they live, as normative.*[79]

---

[78] Frank C. Senn, *The Witness of the Worshiping Community: Liturgy and the Practice of Evangelism* (Paulist Press, 1993) p.28.

[79] Robert Banks, *Paul's Idea of Community: The Early House Churches in Their Historical Setting* (Eerdmans, 1980) p.92.

Participating in the future of God's reign, all of life becomes 'eucharist,' a movement of love and adoration towards God, the movement in which alone the meaning and the value of all that exists can be revealed and fulfilled.[80] Christians worship so that all of life might become worship.

Worship as A Grateful Acknowledgement of Reality

Worship "in spirit and truth" (John 4:23) engages the imagination. It is mind-expanding in that it enables believers to transcend their immediate situation, to envision and dream, to see "a new heaven and a new earth." Here is the true meaning of worship, its power of judgment and transformation in a God-centered view of reality. Not an experience of introspective piety, private devotion, or superficial escape, the church worships so that it may truly see the world. God is at work in all of life, "but humanity is a blinded race, and in worship we have a chance to look on the world in its full, transparent reality – as the place of God's love and activity."[81] Thus worship is not retreat from the world, but an exercise in vision which discerns God's redemptive presence: "with the eyes of your heart enlightened, you may know the hope to which he has called you" (Eph. 1:18). Within the worship of the church the world is liberated and restored to its rightful place as God's sacramental creation: "the sign and means of God's presence and wisdom, love and revelation."[82]

Worship as Forming a People of the Kingdom

Through worship individuals are shaped and formed into a particular people-a people of the kingdom, living a new ethic – the ethic of the kingdom. Open to and embracing the gift and the promise of life within the realm of God's gracious and liberating rule, this people is formed into a witnessing community of gratitude and obedience, of service and sacrifice, of praise and commitment, of freedom and responsibility. The church is itself a "sacrament of the kingdom" which symbolizes the communion of all human beings in God's new creation. In its worship the church acknowledges the fallenness and alienation of the world, celebrates the world's recreation through the event of Jesus Christ, and in the joy and peace of the Holy Spirit manifests the "first fruits" of the fulfillment of the destiny of the world.

Modern secularism is not just a contemporary movement to which the church must accommodate its ministry and its worship; it is a lie and distortion which views the world as an end in itself. Rather than seeing the world as a sacrament of communion with God, the world becomes the ultimate reference point of existence – it becomes humanity's god. Within this idolatrous context, humanity ceases to be the "priest" of God's creation and becomes the world's slave. As a kingdom people immersed in "a movement of love and

---

[80] Schmemann, *For the Life of the World,* p.34.

[81] Robert E. Webber and Rodney Clapp, *People of the Truth: A Christian Challenge to Contemporary Culture* (Morehouse Publishing, 1993) p.94.

[82] Schmemann, *For the Life of the World,* p.14.

adoration," the church offers an alternative perspective by symbolizing the distinctive social reality of the reign of God. The eschatological witness of the worshiping community is to announce and to embody the loving and reconciling society of God's new creation in the midst of the injustice, estrangement, despair, and violence of modem society. What the world needs from the church is not a reflection of itself, but the witness to and proclamation of God's "mighty acts."

> *What the Church brought into the world was not certain ideas applicable simply to human needs, but first of all the truth, the righteousness, the joy of the Kingdom of God.*[83]

[83] Alexander Schmemann, *Sobomost 7* (1985).

QUESTIONS FOR REFLECTION AND DISCUSSION

1. What does it mean to say that the moral witness of Christian communities is eschatological?

2. How does worship relate to the church's moral witness?

3. How is the worship of your church an exercise in vision?

4. How does worship as forming a people of the kingdom relate to your understanding and experience of worship?

BIBLIOGRAPHY

Arias, Mortimer. *Announcing the Reign of God: Evangelization and the Subversive Memory of Jesus.* Fortress Press, 1984.

Banks, Robert. *Paul's Idea of Community: The Early House Churches in Their Historical Setting.* Eerdmans, 1980.

Bellah, Robert, et al. *Habits of the Heart: Individualism and Commitment in American Life.* University of California Press, 1983.

Burkhard, John E. *Worship: A Searching Examination of the Liturgical Experience.* Westminster Press, 1982.

Clapp, Rodney. *Families At The Crossroads: Beyond Traditional and Modern.* InterVarsity Press, 1983.

Dykstra, Craig. *Growing in the Life of Christian Faith.* Theology and Worship Ministry Unit, Presbyterian Church (U.S.A.), 1989.

____________."No Longer Strangers: The Church and Its Educational Ministry." *Princeton Seminary Bulletin.* 6:3 (Nov. 1985): 169.

____________."Reconceiving Practice." *Shifting Boundaries: Contextual Approaches to the Structure of Theological Education.* Barbara Wheeler and Edward Farley, eds. Westminster/John Knox Press, 1991.

____________. *Vision and Character: A Christian Educator's Alternative to Kohlberg.* Paulist Press, 1981.

Fowl Stephen E. and L. Gregory Jones. *Reading in Community: Scripture and Ethics in Christian Life.* Eerdmans, 1991.

Gish, Arthur G. *Living in Christian Community.* Herald Press, 1979.

Hanson, R.P.C. "The Divinity of the Holy Spirit." *Church Quarterly.* Aug. 1969.

Hauerwas, Stanley. *Against the Nations: War and Survival in a Liberal Society.* University of Notre Dame Press, 1992.

____________. *Character and the Christian Life.* Trinity University Press, 1975.

____________. *Christian Existence Today: Essays on Church, World, and Living in Between.* The Labyrinth Press, 1988.

Hauerwas, Stanley and William H. Willimon. *Resident Aliens: Life in the Christian Colony.* Abingdon Press, 1989.

Jennings, Theodore W. *The Liturgy of Liberation: The Confession and Forgiveness of Sins*. Abingdon, 1988,

Jones, L. Gregory. *Transformed Judgment: Toward A Trinitarian Account of the Moral Life.* University of Notre Dame, 1990.

Kasemann, Ernst. *Essays on New Testament Themes.* Fortress Press, 1964.

Kung, Hans. *The Church.* Image Books, 1976.

Lohmeyer, Ernst. *"Our Father": An Introduction to the Lord's Prayer.* Harper & Row, 1952.

Long, D. Stephen. *Living the Discipline.* Eerdmans, 1992.

MacIntyre, Alasdair. *After Virtue: A Study in Moral Theology.* University of Notre Dame Press, 1984.

McClendon, James Wm. *Systematic Theology: Doctrine. Vol. II.* Abingdon Press, 1994.

____________. *Systematic Theology: Ethics. Vol. I.* Abingdon Press, 1986.

Meeks, Wayne. *The Origins of Christian Morality.* Yale University Press, 1993.

Norgren, William A. and William G. Rusch, eds. *Implications of the Gospel: Lutheran Episcopal Dialogue, Series II.* Augsburg Fortress, 1988.

Pannenberg, Wolfhart. *Christian Spirituality.* Westminster Press, 1983.

____________. *Theology and the Kingdom of God.* Westminster Press, 1977.

Russell, Keith A. *In Search of the Church: New Testament Images for Tomorrow's Congregations.* Alban Institute, 1994.

Schmemann, Alexander. *For the Life of the World: Sacraments and Orthodoxy.* St. Vladimir's Seminary Press, 1973.

Senn, Frank C. *The Witness of the Worshiping Community: Liturgy and the Practice of Evangelism.* Paulist Press, 1993.

Wallis, Jim. *Agenda for A Biblical People: A New Focus for Developing A Life-Style of Discipleship* (Harper & Row, 1976).

____________. *The Call to Conversion: Recovering the Gospel for These Times.* Harper, 1992.

Warren, Michael. *Faith, Culture, and the Worshiping Community.* Paulist Press, 1989.

Webber, Robert E. and Rodney, Clapp. *The People of the Truth: A Christian Challenge to Contemporary Culture.* Morehouse Publishing, 1993.

Westerhoff, John H. *Building God's People In A Materialistic Society.* Seabury Press, 1983.

___________. *Living the Faith Community: The Church That Makes A Difference.* Harper & Row, 1986.

Westerhoff, John H. and William H. Willimon. *Liturgy and Learning Through the Life Cycle.* Seabury Press, 1980.

Williams, Raymond. *Key Words: A Vocabulary of Culture and Society.* Oxford University Press, 1976.

Williams, Rowan. *Resurrection.* The Pilgrim Press, 1982.

___________. "Trinity and Revelation." *Modern Theology.* 2:3, 1986.

Willimon, William H. *The Service of God: How Worship and Ethics are Related.* Abingdon Press, 1983.

___________. *What's Right With the Church.* Harper & Row, 1985.

Yannaras, Christos. *The Freedom of Morality.* St. Vladimir's Seminary Press, 1984.

Yoder, John Howard. *Body Politics: Five Practices of the Christian Community Before the Watching World.* Discipleship Resources, 1993.

___________. *The Original Revolution.* Herald Press, 1977.

___________. *The Royal Priesthood: Essays Ecclesiological and Ecumenical.* Michael G. Cartwright, ed. Eerdmans, 1994.

Zizoulas, John D. *Being as Communion.* St. Vladimir's Seminary Press, 1985.

DISCERNING GOD'S VISION FOR THE CHURCH
Congregational Study Resources

What Is God calling the church to be and do in the midst of an increasingly secular world? To enable a guided study of God's call and God's vision for the church the Center has created several study resources for use by church leadership groups. These resources engage people in substantive but accessible theological inquiry and conversation. Participants become grounded in scripture and tradition as they take the time to consider basic aspects of Christianity. The resources assume that only the people of God can discern the 'mind' of God and seek to cultivate a learning community as participants explore, share, and strengthen their common faith and shared ministry. Current publications include:

The People Called by God. This Bible study explores three biblical images of the church: the People of God, the Body of Christ, and the Communion of the Holy Spirit. The eleven session study includes integrating exercises and suggestions for study group facilitators. Through their study of the identity and purpose of the church within scripture, participants begin to identity the dynamic and creative characteristics of Christian community.

Behold: There is a New Creation! This six session Bible study explores the powerful biblical image of new creation -- one of the principal images by which the early church understood its nature and mission. This study follows God's vision for creation from the beginning to the end of the biblical witness and helps participants to clarify the role and mission of the church in light of that vision. This is a substantive while accessible Bible study in which each session offers an introduction and study process as well as options for additional reflection and discussion.

A People of Salt and Light: Jesus' Model for Community. This six session Bible study explores such topics as the blessings of the reign of God, Jesus' vision of right relationships, the practices of Christian faithfulness, and today's church as a contrast community. Questions for reflection and discussion help to focus discussion on the implications of Jesus' vision for their congregation.

We Believe: Shaping and Sharing Christian Belief. This 12 session study engages participants in dialogue with the church's heritage as they consider the boundaries and content of an appropriate and relevant expression of faith in today's church. Integrating exercises, recommendations for study group facilitators, and suggestions for discovering how their congregation shapes and shares Christian belief are included. This study invites participants to investigate, and interpret the Nicene Creed as a powerful and living expression of the church's confession of praise and thanksgiving to God.

Teach Us to Pray: Nurturing Christian Prayer. This 12 session study enables participants to share their current understanding and practice of prayer as they explore the context, content, and purpose of the foundational prayer of the church: the Lord's Prayer. Integrating exercises, aids for study group facilitators, and suggestions for discovering how prayer is nurtured within their congregation are included. Participants broaden and deepen their understanding of prayer as an *ecclesial* practice which is "learned" through involvement in the prayerful life of Christian community.

The Beatitudes: The Practice of Christian Community. This 10 session Bible study explores the Beatitudes in the Gospel of Matthew as the distinctive 'ethic' or way of life to be found within Christian community. Integrating exercises and suggestions for utilizing this study in an envisioning process are included. Participants will discover that as a community of disciples they are called to live the way of life taught by and embodied in Jesus Christ and thus to participate in the blessings found in a faithful and obedient relationship with God.

The Church and the Coming Reign of God. This six session Bible study explores the mission of the church as a sign, foretaste, and instrument of the coming reign of God. Within the context of the kingdom or reign of God as the vision of what God creates the world to be, participants will engage the Bible as a book of visions which inspires and supports hopes and dreams. This Bible study will make an important contribution to a congregational visioning process.

The Biblical Mission of the Church. This four session Bible study facilitates discernment by studying Jesus' final charge or commissioning of the disciples within each of the four gospels. To gain a richer understanding of the mission of the church, each 'commission' is placed within the context and content of the full Gospel of which it is the climax.

The Practice of Sabbath Time. This study resource provides a wonderful starting point for developing a new inventiveness around "remembering the Sabbath day." It offers an insightful study of four practices of Sabbath keeping: the Trust of Ceasing; the Faith of Resting; the Joy of Embracing; and the Hope of Feasting. Many examples, illustrations, and ideas for keeping Sabbath are drawn from several cultures and are provided to stimulate creativity in your church. The footnotes and suggestions for further reading help to link the study group participants with the wider body of Christian communities.

Gathered Together to Seek and to Do God's Will. The goal of this study resource is to enable decision making to become a theologically responsible process that shapes and expresses Christian faith. This resource explores an approach to decision making that moves beyond win/lose competitive struggles to a way of seeking wisdom together and agreement about God's will for shared life and mutual ministry. Using Acts 10-15 as an illustration of early church decision making, this study includes a process for exploring your church's narrative of decision making, and offers a guide for planning to become more fully a "wisdom community."

Cultivating Missional Communities. This resource explores the cultivation of missional communities by focusing upon Christian "practices," those communal behaviors which shape, teach, train, equip – cultivate – the identity, vision, and mission of Christian communities. Thus worship, prayer, baptism eucharist, decision-making, forgiveness are not simply religious goods and services offered to individuals, but practices through which a people are formed in a distinctive way of life.

For more Information or for ordering these and other church transformation resources, contact:
The Center for Parish Development, www.missionalchurch.org.
1448 E. 53rd Street, Chicago, IL 60615. 773-752-1596. Fax: 773-752-5093